An Early Career Book

careers in an
AIRPLANE FACTORY

OBSOLETE

Rivian Bell and Teresa Koenig

photographs by
Glen Sunderland and Bob Ferguson
Lockheed-California Company

Lerner Publications Company
Minneapolis, Minnesota

LIBRARY OF CONGRESS CATALOGING IN PUBLICATION DATA

Bell, Rivian.
Careers in an airplane factory.

(An Early career book)
Summary: Describes fifteen different career possibilities within a large airplane factory including such occupations as riveter, research engineer, designer, and plant manager.

1. Airplanes — Design and construction — Vocational guidance — Juvenile literature. [1. Airplanes — Design and construction — Vocational guidance. 2. Vocational guidance] I. Koenig, Teresa. II. Sunderland, Glen, ill. III. Ferguson, Robert, 1921-   , ill. IV. Title. V. Series.

TL671.28.B39   629.134′023   82-17136
ISBN 0-8225-0349-2 (lib. bdg.)

International Standard Book Number: 0-8225-0349-2   Library of Congress Catalog Card Number: 82-17136

1 2 3 4 5 6 7 8 9 10 92 91 90 89 88 87 86 85 84 83

Would you like to work in an airplane factory?

In 1903, Orville and Wilbur Wright made the first successful flight in an airplane. That flight lasted less than one minute, but it paved the way for the future of the airplane. Today, many people travel by airplane. Airplanes are also used as a quick way to send freight and mail all over the world.

It takes many years to design a new airplane and more than one year to build one. In the following pages, you will learn about some of the many people who work in a large airplane factory. Each of these people has an important job to do in helping to build planes that are safe and comfortable.

PROPOSAL PERSON

Because airplanes are so expensive, the airplane factory does not begin building an airplane until a customer has ordered it. Some of the customers are airline companies, who use the planes to carry passengers. Other customers are the governments of the United States and other countries, who buy the planes for military use.

The proposal person talks with each customer to find out what kind of plane is needed and when it must be ready. He or she then writes a report, or *proposal*, that contains all of the facts about the plane, including the price. If the customer accepts the proposal, the factory will begin working on the plane.

A proposal person must have several different skills. He or she must be a good salesperson and must be able to work with numbers and to write legal contracts.

DESIGNER

Every part in a new airplane must be designed before the part can be made. Each large section of a plane, such as the engine, the wing, or the cockpit, is made up of smaller parts. Because there are so many parts in a plane, many designers work on different sections of the plane at the same time.

A designer first decides how a plane part should work. He or she then draws a picture of what the finished part should look like. Instead of drawing with paper and pencils, the designer uses a computer screen and a special pen called a *light pen*. The light pen uses light instead of lead or ink. This picture shows a designer drawing on a screen with a light pen.

To design parts that will work, airplane designers must know how planes are made and how they fly. When the designers finish their drawings, they send them to the draftsperson.

DRAFTSPERSON

Based on the designers' drawings for each part, the drafts-person draws *blueprints* of the new airplane. Blueprints are detailed pictures that show how to build the plane. In this picture, the draftsperson is using a special machine to draw a huge blueprint. When it is finished, this plan will show how the sections of the plane fit together.

A draftsperson must have an eye for detail and must be able to draw and measure accurately. He or she must also learn how to use many kinds of drawing equipment, such as special rulers and triangles.

127790

RESEARCH CHEMIST

Research chemists are always looking for better materials to use in building planes. Some of an airplane's parts, such as those close to the jet engines, must be able to stand extremely high temperatures. Other parts must be very lightweight. Research chemists must find the best material, such as plastic, glass, or metal, for each part.

Research chemists also test materials already being used in planes. They experiment to find more efficient fuels to power planes. And if an airplane part breaks, they try to find out why. In this picture, a chemist is using a computer to analyze a material. Maybe he will be able to make the material stronger so that the part will not break again.

People who want to become research chemists must spend several years studying chemistry, physics, and other science subjects.

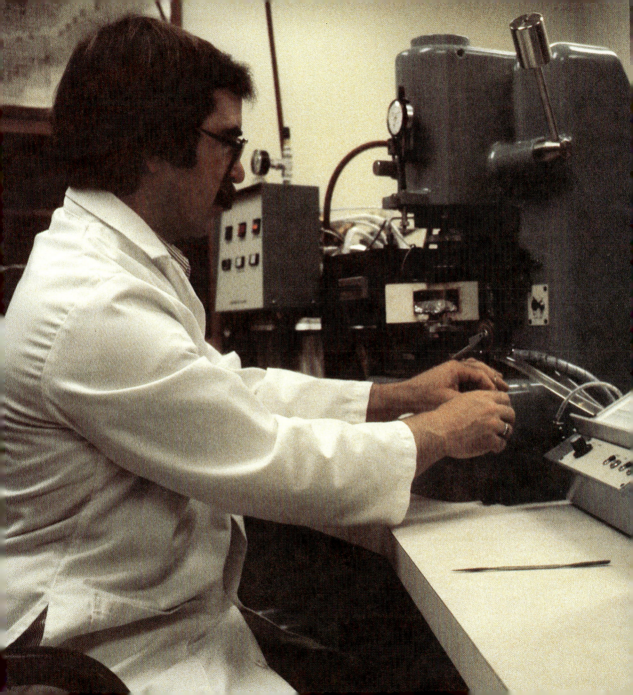

METALLURGIST

Like the research chemist, the metallurgist (met-uhl-ER-jist) tries to find new and better materials for building airplanes. But unlike the research chemist, the metallurgist only works with metals.

The body of an airplane is all metal. This metal must be strong enough to withstand very hot temperatures and very cold ones. It must also last through all kinds of weather. The tiniest weakness in the metal could cause a part to break. The metallurgist must make sure this does not happen.

The metallurgist in this picture is testing a piece of metal. First he puts it into an *electron microscope*, which enlarges the image of the metal to thousands of times its actual size. Then he photographs it. After the piece of metal has been heated to a high temperature, he puts it back in the microscope. Next he compares the new picture, shown on the screen, with the photograph, and looks for any cracks that the heat may have caused.

STRUCTURAL ENGINEER

A model of every section of a new airplane must be tested before the factory can actually make the parts for it. The structural engineer is in charge of these tests. He or she works in a very large laboratory like the one in the picture.

Some tests take up to four years. The structural engineer will *simulate*, or copy, 20 years' worth of weather and other flight conditions. In this picture, part of the tail fin is being tested. Huge valves will press up on the fin to see how it will react to air pressure.

The structural engineer must make sure that each section of the new plane will be safe. If he or she discovers a problem, the section will be taken apart. Then the parts that don't work will be sent back to the research chemist, the metallurgist, or the research engineer to be improved.

RESEARCH ENGINEER

Some research engineers at an airplane factory work on ways to improve the factory so that planes can be built faster. They invent different kinds of robots. Some of these robots can move airplane parts from one area of the factory to another. The mechanical arm that picked up rocks on the moon was designed by a research engineer.

Other engineers invent new systems to use in the planes, such as automatic warning systems and navigational systems. Like designers, research engineers design the programs that tell the robots how to make the parts for the new systems that the engineers are inventing. Here an engineer looks at an old part to see if he can modify it. Using a light pen, the research engineer can tell the robot what to do with the part.

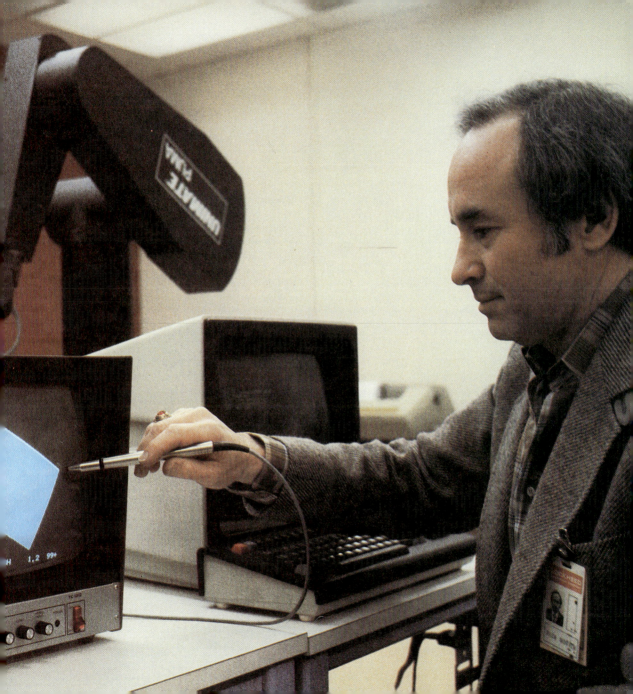

COMPUTER ANALYST

Computer analysts serve every department in an airplane factory. In fact, the computer center is much like a library. All of the information from different parts of the factory is stored there.

A computer analyst helps people who use the computer. They repair computers for the engineers and scientists. They work with the people in the accounting department to keep track of the costs for each plane. And when people need to use a computer for a new project, the computer analyst sets up a program and explains how to use it.

Working with computers requires special training. To be a good computer analyst, one must also like to solve problems.

ELECTRICAL SPECIALIST

All of the important controls and lights in an airplane run on electricity. Electrical specialists hook together the electrical systems on airplanes.

Electrical specialists must know a great deal about how electricity works. They work with small tools to connect hundreds of wires together. To know exactly what kind and what amount of wire to use, the electrical specialists study printed instructions called *wire cards*. Wire cards show each part of the plane's wiring design.

Before they can work in an airplane factory, electrical specialists must first learn about electricity. Most electrical specialists begin their careers by working in a small electrical shop.

RIVETER

The outside of an airplane is made of sheets of metal called *skins*. Like the skin on our bodies, airplane skins are very thin. They are held together by *rivets*, which are similar to nails but weigh much less. The riveter is responsible for putting together all of the skins.

To know where to put the rivets, riveters follow patterns. In this picture, the rivet patterns are already in position. The riveter is using a special gun to force the rivets through the holes in the metal. To hold the rivet gun in place, a riveter must be strong and steady.

UPHOLSTERER

After the frame of an airplane has been finished, it must be upholstered with insulating material. Upholsterers, like the woman in this picture, cut each piece of insulation and fit it inside the frame. This material will be covered by the inside walls and will help to keep the inside of the plane from getting too hot or too cold.

Upholsterers also cover the airplane seats with padding and cloth. When the body of the plane is ready, other workers lay the carpet and install the seats, window shades, lights, and overhead racks.

FLIGHT LINE MECHANIC

The last people to check a new airplane before its test flight are the flight line mechanics. These mechanics check the fuel tank to make sure that it is full. Then they check the electrical systems to be sure that all of the wires are connected properly. They also check the air conditioning and heating systems to be sure they are working.

An airplane factory has several flight line mechanics, each with different duties. Those that perform the most important tasks must be licensed by the government to do their work.

TEST PILOT

Before a finished plane is delivered to the customer, it is flown by a test pilot. All of the airplane's instruments, parts, and controls have already been tested by machines and people on the ground. It is the test pilot, though, who finds out if the airplane can actually fly. This can be a risky job.

Test pilots must have many years of flying experience. That way, they will know right away if a part of the plane is not working correctly during a flight. If something is wrong, the test pilot will tell the designers and engineers about the problem. When the test pilot says the airplane is safe to fly, the airplane is ready for delivery to the customer.

PLANT MANAGER

The plant manager is in charge of all of the other workers at the airplane factory. He or she meets with many different workers each day. Sometimes the plant manager looks at the work of the designers. Other times the plant manager talks with the proposal person about the costs of a plane or discusses a new idea with the research engineer.

The plant manager must see that nothing goes wrong on the assembly line where the airplane is being put together. If something does go wrong, however, the manager must also be able to solve the problem.

INDUSTRIAL RECREATION INSTRUCTOR

Managers have learned that people work together better when they feel good about themselves. To help with this, many large factories employ an industrial recreation instructor to plan sports activities for the workers. The instructors hold physical fitness classes, like the one shown here. They also organize league games before or after work.

Because so many people work in an airplane factory, these recreation programs are very important. They help develop team spirit among the workers so that working together becomes easier. People who come to the sports activities have fun meeting employees from different parts of the factory. Softball, bowling, basketball, and golf are popular sports among airplane workers.

Airplane factory careers described in this book

Proposal Person

Designer

Draftsperson

Research Chemist

Metallurgist

Structural Engineer

Research Engineer

Computer Analyst

Electrical Specialist

Riveter

Upholsterer

Flight Line Mechanic

Test Pilot

Plant Manager

Industrial Recreation Instructor

The publisher would like to thank Lockheed-California Company,
Burbank, California, for its cooperation in the preparation of
this book.

Lerner Publications Company
241 First Avenue North, Minneapolis, Minnesota 55401